WINDOW TO MY WORLD

Also by Parvati Anil
Paths Intertwined (2026)

WINDOW TO MY WORLD

Parvati Anil

BOOKSTHAKAM KIDS

Published by Bookstakam Kids, an imprint of
Cogitabund LLP

publishing@cogitabund.com
www.cogitabund.com

Window to My World

A Cogitabund Book/ published by arrangement with the author

ISBN: 978-93-49383-35-7

Typeset and Cover Design by Cogitabund LLP
Printed and bounded in India by Manipal Technologies Limited

MIX Paper | Supporting responsible forestry FSC® C043100

Cogitabund LLP is committed to a sustainable future of our business, our readers and our planet. This book is made from Forest Stewardship Council® certified paper.

"To my parents, who never stopped encouraging me and for being with me every step of the way. For letting me chase my vivid imaginations and helping me to reach my best. To my brother who inspired me to start writing poems".

Contents

Friends	1
What the waves talked to the shore	2
My little sister	3
Flowers	4
A star with a wing and a heart	5
The mist was not happy to say good morning to dawn	6
Blue prints	7
A dog without a tail	8
Aliens	9
The Stars	10
Bloom	11
The Sun	12
Dear Mr Examiner	13
It's time to come	15
Wandering without reason	16
Ballerina	17
A tale of two lovers	18
Our dear Mother stream	20
Sleep Tight	22
A new land	23
The Dance of the Dandelion seeds	25
A lovely boy	26
Cheating	28
The Lilly	30
A world unravelled	31
One so vast	33
My dear sweet mother	35

WINDOW TO MY WORLD

Foreword

Parvati Anil's book of poems, Window to my World' is a delicate poetry collection, aptly titled. Indeed, the twenty seven poems in the collection, are twenty seven windows into Parvati Anil's world of poetry. The poems reveal a tender poet at work, who is loving, kind, compassionate, and unselfish. Parvati's mind is abundant with caring, sharing, forgiveness, and tenderness, values that get skillfully reflected in her poems. The poems show her keen powers of observation and creative perception.

A poem such as 'A Dog without a Tail' can be very touching. The poem reveals the young poet's ability to feel and understand the lives and sufferings of others. It is a great quality, and the mark of a true poet.

'My Little Sister' shows the poet's contemplative phase, where she analyses herself, ponders over her own weaknesses, and overcomes them, filling her mind with love. The poet's innocence opens petals of pristine poetic beauty. We begin to love the poet- child.

Poetry is a healing agent for Parvati that lets her be at peace with herself. At times of self doubts or in times of difficulty, her poetry becomes her best friend and she works her way with her poems to find solutions for her troubled heart.

Parvati's obvious gift for poetry makes her utter profound truths as 'As long as we have memories/ yesterday remains / As long as we have hope/ Tomorrow awaits.' (Friends). In the poem ' What the Waves Talked to the Shore, the poet innocently asks a question that sums up the mystery of our lives 'Why was it with cool breeze/that the waves come to touch the shore/ Why do they carry away a part of the shore as they go?

'The Mist Was not Happy to say Good Morning to the Dawn' is a moving poem about the transience of life and the need to cultivate acceptance in our lives, observing examples from nature. It says a poignantly delicate story of 'mist' that is happy with friends such as cherries, but must soon leave. The idea in the poem is unique, and the lines are well crafted , such that the poem stays on with the reader.

The poet's subtle sense of humour comes deftly through in the poem ' Dear Mr Examiner.' The poem is easily one of the finest in the collection and shows the poets wide range of perception, analysis of human behaviour, her powers of observation, sense of poetic craft, and also reveals her emerging maturity as a poet.

It has been a pleasure reading the book of poems ' Window to my World' by Parvati Anil. I wish the young poet- heart great laurels ahead, and close with a quote from the poet's lines from the poem 'Sleep- Tight' 'Hush now, little babe, tight/ For tomorrow you are going to be a star.'

— Gopikrishnan Kottoor

Preface

"The ideas for my poems always come unexpectedly. When I write, I seem to enter a world of fantasy, and endless thoughts fill my mind. I have my family to thank for encouraging me again and again not to waste my imagination and to aspire to write more. I thank all my readers for spending a little time with my imagination, and I hope I have inspired you to unleash your creativity. Thank you for picking up my book. It is my first collection of poems, and it is very special to me. I hope you will enjoy reading it as much as I enjoyed writing it."

— Parvati Anil

Acknowledgement

A heartfelt thanks to my mom for putting in endless effort to turning my dream book to reality and also for her whole hearted support that she gives me. Without her, the book or its illustrations won't have been possible. I would like to thank my father and my brothers too for their help and also to my extended family for believing in me so that I could write better poetry.

And a special thanks to Booksthakam and the team who worked hard to make my dream a reality.

Friends

Friends are like stars,
You can't always see them.
But you know they are there.
Always and forever.

As long as we have memories,
Yesterday remains.
As long as we have hope,
Tomorrow awaits.
As long as we have friendship,
Each day is never a waste.

1 cup of sharing,
2 cups of caring,
1 cup of forgiveness and
Hugs of tenderness.
Mix all these together…
To make friends forever…

What the waves talked to the shore

I once had a little wonder,
What the waves talked to the shore.
Why was it with cool breeze
That the waves come to touch the sandy shore?
Why do they carry away a part of the shore as they go?
What are they saying to each other, I wonder.
Maybe they talked about people coming
To happily enjoy them.
Maybe they are thinking of staying together.
Maybe, just maybe they wish to take
Rest from the people that come.
Why doesn't the waves stay with the shore?
Why do they go away?
Maybe they want to stay, but could not.
Oh ! how I wonder
What the waves talked to the shore.

My little sister

My little sister, fair as she may be.
She is naughty, but kind.
Beautiful as she is brave.
Though we may have differences,
And though we fight all week long,
She has a place in my heart.
We might fight,
But what is the fun in not fighting,
With a beloved sibling.
Adults may or may not understand that.
But if they do, they will know
They went through that too.
When my little sister came,
I was jealous.
But I need not be.
Cause sharing things with someone
Is better than being alone.
So my little sister has a special place in my heart,
And I know I have a place in hers too.

Flowers

Flowers are a mystery.
For no one knows,
How or why they bloom at times.
Some at dawn,
Some late at night,
Like a flickering light.
Cause no one knows when it blooms,
Or when it closes its petals.
Flowers can be shy,
But they will show their bloom to the world outside.
They lift their petals, oh so gracefully.
But flowers remain a mystery.
It carries throughout history.
Some at ten, some at noon.
Some bloom throughout the seasons hues.
That is why flowers are a mystery.

A star with a wing and a heart

I once saw a little star in the sky.
The most exciting thing was that
It was a star with a wing and a heart!
As the star passed over my house,
I asked it "Oh star, Oh little star,
Why do you have a wing so small
And a heart so bright ?"
The star replied so gracefully,
"Oh little boy, don't be amazed .
Cause all of us have a wing and heart.
Our hearts so bright is what you see,
When you look up at the midnight sky.
Our little wings help us move around,
And look after the children of this joyful earth".

The mist was not happy to say good morning to dawn

The mist was not happy to say good morning to dawn.
Cause he would have to go away
From his cheery friends, the flowers,
And the jumping critters
That move at night with help from him.
He hates to leave at dawn but he must.
Sometimes the mist might stay longer than he should,
For he could not bear to leave his friends.
The dawn felt sorry for the mist,
But he knew they must be on time.
But once a year the sun delays,
And the mist with his cheery friends
Play all night long.
So children looking out the window at dawn wonder ,
Why the mist was not happy to say good morning to dawn.

Blue prints

I always had a wonder,
What makes us look like kin.
Did I inherit my sense of humour,
Or these long legs?
What if I grow tall like my brother,
Or what if I am short?
How long after I start growing,
Until I start to shrink?
Am I going to lose my teeth someday?
My hair, my mind?
Do you think I will be big or thin,
Or bursting at the seam?
Am I naturally this crazy,
Or is it something in my genes?
I am more than who I am.
I am also who I am from.
It is a scary speculation,
Who I will become.

A dog without a tail

I once met a dog without a tail.
I was so surprised to see
That he was still so happy.
I decided to bring him home,
To find out why he had no tail.
He loved my family from the start.
He was just a little joyful dog.
First I found out that it was
Hard to communicate without a tail.
But what my little dog did was,
He started using his tongue alike
With all the other parts around.
He used his mouth and nose and eyes
His head, his ears, his legs alike.
We all love him and his joyful mind.
We all love him to the very best.

Aliens

We got an alien at our school.
He is on an exchange trip.
I quite fancy him,
If he wasn't so weird looking.
He has a head with three eyes,
He is short and has four legs,
He has big furry claws,
And don't laugh, he has two huge feelers .
But as our teacher said to us,
We mustn't laugh at him.
When we first saw him, we fell about
But we have stopped now
Because our teachers said so.
Next week we are visiting the place,
From where our friend had come from .
Its got a funny name,
It's called "Grognak".
I am not looking forward to it,
Because we might be stumbled upon.
Still it will make a change
From the boring school.
And perhaps some aliens will quite fancy me too.

The Stars

When you look up at the night sky,
What do you see?
Those beautiful stars that fill up the sky.
Those stars that make up funny shapes.
Those stars that blink away the darkness of night.
Those stars that light up the sky in the middle of the night.
Those stars that move away for the sun to take their place.
Those grateful stars that we adore are here today.

Bloom

As the sun shines upon the land,
A little flower comes to bloom.
Through its first glance of the outside world,
It knew it would have a happy life.
It grew days at a stretch.
But it always wondered what it means to have a friend.
Unknown to him, an another seed had come to life .
And just like him, she had wondered
What it would be like to have a friend.
Oh if only they would just turn around,
They would know that they had a friend all along.
As they grew, so did their loneliness
They grew sad with despair.
But once as a child passed them by.
She said "Oh these sad flowers.
If only they knew that they had
A friend by their side all along"
Hearing this the flowers turned,
And met their mate for life.

The Sun

Eastward she arrives,
A flower blooming in the sky.
Little rays peeping
Through the clouds of the sky.
A gentle smile unfolds,
Revealing a mother who cares for all.
Happiness awaits all
Waking to her whispers.
All are her children,
And she their mother.
Dawn till dusk watching over us.
Tired, the mother goes to sleep,
Darkness filling the sky.
But all know to await,
The gentle ray, waking them the next day.
Coming to wake us with her gentle smile,
Lighting our days and clearing our minds.

Dear Mr Examiner

Your questions were lovely.
I have read them carefully through.
But there isn't a single one of them
That I know the answer to.
My name and date are written,
As beautifully as I could.
Now I have nothing further to say,
Than the year, the month, the day.
So I thought that I would write you a letter,
Quite informal, but fair.
About what I can see from my desk here,
And what is it like to be me.
My friend has written 10 pages,
But it is probably just doodles.
And my enemy over there
Is copying the answers off his cuff.
Our teacher is marking our homework.
The clock keeps ticking away.
I suppose for anyone outside our school,
It's just a normal day .
There will be mothers going on errands.
Grandmothers sipping tea.
Unemployed men doing crossword
Or watching movies on tv.
The rain has finally stopped here.
The sun has started to shine.
And in a back garden in our lane,
A maid hangs shirts on a line.
A class flies past to play tennis.

I am sure their stress is over.
A mower chugs back and forth,
Up on the football field.
Our teacher just read what I have written.
Her face is an absolute mark.
Before she collects the papers in,
I have a tiny favour to ask.
I thought your questions were lovely,
I have only myself to blame.
But could you give me some marks,
For writing the date and my name.

It's time to come

The moonlight peeks its way through the rocks,
To the humble abode in which I live.
Waiting on a miracle I've wished for long.
A miracle in which you come to my side.
Long has it been, the last we met.
When your cold sweet rain showered me with joy.
You have enemies a handful who drive us apart,
But nothing can keep us from reuniting.
Prayers and prayers I have sent to you,
Asking where art thou my dear friend.
Leave your troubles and sorrows behind,
Cause it's time to come and dance with me.
Withering away will I, in the scorching sun of summer.
But I will be standing here waiting for you to return.
When the clouds come back to block her rays,
Will I know you came to me.
Leave your troubles and sorrows behind,
Cause it's time to come and reunite again.

Wandering without reason

I am hungry in Hungary.
I prance through France.
I roam through Rome.
And saw geese in Greece.

What but these sayings can fulfil a poet's dream.
Words to wisdom with creativity at brim,
But no one knows what yet to become.
Those glimmering sayings that hang in my mind,
And what yet to be may not be known,
As the number of lines start to rise.

As dawn breaks upon us will they only be understood.
But the sayings hold a worthy hand
Upon my faithful mind.
Only then will thy sayings be truthfully mine.

Those words so wise can still be sweet,
Fluttering into my mind, like a sweet gentle breeze.
It may be deep inside us, but to bring it to light,
We must be truthfully kind.

Those words of wisdom are truly mine,
As I journeyed around Hungary, France, Rome and
Greece…

Ballerina

As silent as a feather being blown away by air,
A ballerina tiptoes to the centre of the stage.
Forgetting her troubles, she enthrals us with wonders.
Wonders too majestic to forget.
Impossible are these miraculous feats to one.
Knowing no other world, she'll frolic till the end.
One word to call those who perform this feat.
Ballerina, oh what a word it turned out to be.
Years and years it takes to master this art.
But smiles will never fade, as she first enters the stage.
Through her actions and poise,
Ballerina shows us the true art that is ballet.
To come upon this marvel, we are to be blessed.
Ballerinas are the true souls of ballet.

A tale of two lovers

All have read the tale of two lovers,
By the poet great of time.
A love story led to tragedy.
A peaceful reunion at last.
From two friends, there rose a fight.
Supremacy declaring its leader.
Years and years lasts a feud,
A feud between the two.
From fights so major to feuds so small,
Found were the reason for their hatred to grow.
It went on and on from kin to kin.
Sharing the stories that once were told.
But through all the odds, a love was made.
A love between the two.
A blissful love in between secrets,
A truth that no one knew.
Happiness does not last for long.
For soon troubles came their way.
Two separate lovers,
Fighting for solutions,
To reunite once again .
At last a plan came to one,
A plan that would seal their fate forever.
Letters and letters were sent to the other,
Hoping he had understood .
But woe came to one,
Thinking his love had departed.
He lies on his love with an empty vial in hand.
But alas his lover awoke saying,

"Have you left none for me?"
Their families join together,
Drowned with sadness they stand.
The feud at last was done.
So they can cherish their children in peace.
Such was the tale of two lovers.

Our dear Mother stream

As soft as the wind she flows,
Our dear mother stream,
To a faraway land in which
One can dream.
Hidden in the depths,
Middle of somewhere new,
Rose a tiny trickle,
Waiting to grow up.
One by one her siblings and friends
Joined hands with our little mother stream.
Off they go to a new start in life,
Filled with joy as they take off
To astounding new lands.
Hoping to prosper,
With few new friends in hand.
Troubles arise as one can see,
A barrier of wood obstructing their path.
But our mother stream knew
This shall be her path in life.
One by one they joined their forces
To overcome the one that blocked their path.
Soon it turned out be an successful undertaking,
Blasting the barrier to smithereens, she goes.
As to overcome your troubles is just a way of life.
Soon she became a mother to all.
From elephants to beavers and all creatures the same.
Lending help she goes afar,
Where some shall not know,
Where her beauty ends.

But her secret is known to some critters
Of her unrevealed admirer,
Who protects her whenever she is tired.
With no disturbances, at last she shall go
To the one true love of her life.
The mother stream protects us.
Consider a duty to save her too.
Who she was is known to none,
But to us, shall forever be known
As 'Our dear mother stream'.

Sleep Tight

Hush now, little baby tight .
For tomorrow you are going to be a star,
Sleep tight in your bed little one,
Tomorrow you are going to be okay.
Have a good night sleep little one,
For tomorrow you are going to be the light.
Sleep tight little one tonight,
For tomorrow you're going to be all right.

A new land

With a friend in hand,
Across to an all new land.
Aboard the airborne plane,
I go into the descending rain.
A strange new land arriving,
On an unexpecting Christmas morning.
A thrilling adventure transpiring,
An indelible day anticipating.
Off we shall depart,
To a day we all await.
Family and friends proceed as one.
Returning with a strong bond established.
As the seasons change,
Summer through autumn,
Counting the days ,we shall be.
Lingering for that Christmas Day.
A day for which none can conceal
The eagerness within their hearts.
Friend by friend, hand in hand,
We shall go to a whole new world .
On a Christmas morn, depart we shall,
To a day that is unequalled
By any coming round.
To a new land we go,
An unforgettable occasion forthcoming.

The Dance of the Dandelion seeds

A special feeling lingering,
One by one they part.
Goodbyes may be sorrow,
But important are their families.
Such is the dance of dandelion seeds,
A wonder to behold.
Our little seed is finally alone,
Wondering where to go.
At last he takes a stand
On a wonderful new land.
Over are his adventures,
His journeys at the end .
Oh! what a role had he,
In the wondrous dance performed.
The dance that enthrals us,
The dance that excites us,
The dance of dandelion seeds,
Oh! what a wonder to behold.

A lovely boy

Up and up he rose,
His first glance of the world,
Being quite a blinding one.
Straight to the sun he looked,
Flinching away in fright.
But alas, what else went wrong ?
Nowhere to be seen,
His loving sweet mother.
He turned and turned,
Looked left and right,
But no, his mom is not to be seen,
Sad he grew, but soon found out
A rather strange phenomenon.
A sun so scorching
Looking down on him,
But inside a shade he was .
At last a tingling feeling
He felt in all his roots,
A soft whisper reached his ear.
At once he turned around,
There stood his majestic mother.
Tall, proud and laughing .
At once shyness and love
Was coming over him like a hurricane.
His cheery mother watching him all along,
Laughing was one thing she couldn't stop.
But she alone knew,
What a lovely boy she had.

Cheating

Cheating be not fair,
As knowledge won't be shared.
From overheard answers,
To copying straight up,
Risk be at an impossible rate.
Trouble by far a million times
More when you are caught.
No relation shall be found,
To the marks you have lost.
But the marks you earned on your own,
Shall then be truly yours.
Exams, a test of your knowledge,
And what you've learnt so far.
Not a matter for the marks,
If it wasn't really yours.
One should realise
The anger of the teacher,
Is not what matters more
But the impending future
That will be put at risk.
So as far as I know,
A rule of life that should be applied,
Is that 'cheating be not fair'.

The Lilly

Oh little flower, oh so shy,
Show your bloom to the world outside.
Lift your petals gracefully,
And open up your heart with glee.
Don't be shy, oh little one,
For tomorrow you're gonna be the best.

A world unravelled

A world shall be unravelling,
When a book is opening.
At first glance, interest strikes.
Then a tug of curiosity won't leave you till the end.
Once made friend,
With the one called a book.
Enthralling things our minds shall behold.
One after another, the words flow in
From a printed page , to your blissful mind.
Page by page will be turned,
With excitement leading the way.
What once was a lifeless creature,
Now turned into one full of life.
It may feel like hours and hours to another.
But ourselves be merged in a portal of two worlds,
One with inescaping reality,
And another where anything is possible.
Action movies be forming in mind.
Whether what shall happen,
Be a mystery or predicted.
Free from worry and thought,
We enter a new world,
Which unravelled in our mind.
Ink on a page is what it is.
But the deep hold they have.
Shall be something unknown to all.
The words fill our mind with joy and hope.

Patience be taught, as word by word we wait,
For a twist up along the road.
A magical place was invented,
To all those who are mesmerised.
To pick up a book and open it with glee,
Shall be the end of sorrow
Or any trouble we have.
Leaving everything behind,
With just some words in hand,
We enter a new world.
A world that shall be unravelled.

One so vast

Our nature's beauty is far too untold.
Parts and bits of her outstanding beauty,
Be shared between two.
But her full beauty, still is unknown,
A vast one she being.
Shelters provided, homes be build,
Inside a one so vast.
Love be spread,
Through every whisper of wind.
Sounds shall flow
In and out of her.
Swaying are her trees,
With an unmatched beauty.
Foes she has, who once
Lived off of her.
The one who she nurtures,
The one who now betrays her .
But her beauty being so outstanding,
Sympathy be felt for her,
Even in a child's heart.
But she is still the one,
Who loves us all,
Even if we hurt her too.
Her mind, so thoughtful,
Arms so nurturing,
Be small in terms
Of her unmatched beauty,
The beauty of one so vast.

My dear sweet mother

When trouble arises with unsolvable mysteries,
One we can count on to make the rest history.
No matter the place, the time, the date,
A hero there is, that has your back.
The one who knows you inside out.
Your distresses be known ,
With just a tingle in mind.
Problems all worked out,
With a trick or sleight of hand.
For even the silliest of reasons,
Comes to us our saviour.
The one who nurtures us,
With unconditional love alike.
Only one name have we,
To call those we adore.
My dear sweet mother.
My biggest hero in the world.
None can compensate,
The loving we shall get
From a hero like our mom,
Who will kill us with all her love.
Words would not be found,
Even in the world's biggest books,
Describing our mothers
True to their nature.
Fights and feuds may break out,
But still we'll have a nurturing mother,
Who cares for us with all her heart.

A sentence uttered, that will change both our hearts,
'I love you my dear sweet mother'.

For My Readers

"Opened wide are 27 windows
To my wild little world
Through each window
A different perspective is shown
Your enjoyment in reading my little poems
Is all it take to bring a smile to me
Travel around mysteries and imaginations
Which I hope has filled your heart"